SOUTHWESTERN INDIAN DESIGNS

Madeleine Orban-Szontagh

DOVER PUBLICATIONS, INC.
New York

*I am most grateful to Steve Rogers of the
Wheelwright Museum of the American Indian in Santa Fe
for letting me look through its wonderful collection
of slides of sand paintings.
The drawings of sand paintings in this book are
based on slides owned by the Museum.*

Copyright © 1992 by Dover Publications, Inc.
All rights reserved under Pan American and International Copyright Conventions.

Published in Canada by General Publishing Company, Ltd., 30 Lesmill Road, Don Mills, Toronto, Ontario.

Published in the United Kingdom by Constable and Company, Ltd., 3 The Lanchesters, 162–164 Fulham Palace Road, London W6 9ER.

Southwestern Indian Designs is a new work, first published by Dover Publications, Inc., in 1992.

DOVER *Pictorial Archive* SERIES

Manufactured in the United States of America
Dover Publications, Inc., 31 East 2nd Street, Mineola, N.Y. 11501

Library of Congress Cataloging-in-Publication Data

Orban-Szontagh, Madeleine.
    Southwestern Indian designs / Madeleine Orban-Szontagh.
        p.   cm.—(Dover pictorial archive series)
    ISBN 0-486-26985-X (pbk.)
    1. Indians of North America—Southwest, New—Art—Pictorial works.   2. Decoration and ornament—Southwest, New—Pictorial works.   I. Title.   II. Series.
E78.S7073   1992
745.4'089970789—dc20   91-40991
                                                                                    CIP

Publisher's Note

The ancient arts of the Native Americans of Arizona and New Mexico—basketry, pottery, weaving, carving, metalwork, leatherwork, sand painting—have survived for many centuries and are still practiced by skilled artisans. Some of the present-day artifacts are little changed in pattern and construction from those of a thousand years ago. The 250 designs recreated by Madeleine Orban-Szontagh in this volume from a wide range of handcrafted works make available a large and diverse artistic heritage for new applications.

Here is a brief guide to the peoples and pueblos identified in the captions:

Acoma: one of the western pueblos, in northwestern New Mexico, situated on high cliffs on a 7000-foot mesa; known for their delicate pottery.

Anasazi: the ancient civilization (from ca. A.D. 100) of which the Pueblo Indians are the modern descendants.

Apache: a formerly major Indian group now dwelling on reservations in Arizona and New Mexico.

Cochiti: one of the central pueblos, on the Rio Grande in north-central New Mexico.

Hohokam: the ancestors of the Pima and Papago Indians; inhabited southeastern Arizona ca. 300 B.C.–A.D. 1400.

Hopi: the most western of the pueblos, in the middle of the Navajo reservation in northeastern Arizona; the most productive craftspeople of all the present-day Pueblo Indians. Their kachinas—doll fetishes representing deities as masked ceremonial dancers—are their best-known artifacts.

Laguna: one of the western pueblos, in northwestern New Mexico; famous for their pottery.

Mimbres: an extinct group from the Rio Mimbres Valley in southern New Mexico.

Navajo: the largest Indian tribe in North America; culturally independent, though related to the Apaches; reservation mostly in northeastern Arizona; makers of perhaps the finest North American Indian textiles.

Papago: tribe inhabiting the Mexico-Arizona border region; related to the Pima.

Pima: tribe from southern Arizona, related to the Papago; both known for their basket designs.

Pueblo: Spanish for "village"; the broad term for the large, culturally related group of village-dwelling Indians of northern New Mexico and Arizona.

San Ildefonso: one of the smallest eastern pueblos, on the Rio Grande in northern New Mexico; known for their excellent pottery.

Santo Domingo: one of the central pueblos, on the Rio Grande in northern New Mexico.

Sikyatki: a pueblo ruin in northeastern Arizona; known for the fine pottery unearthed there.

Zia: one of the central pueblos, in northern New Mexico.

Zuni: one of the western pueblos, on the Arizona–New Mexico border.

Navajo rugs *(Private collection)*.

Navajo rug (*Private collection*).

Navajo rugs (*Private collection*).

Navajo rug (*From* Genuine Navajo Rugs *by Noël Bennett*).

Kachina dolls (*Private collection*).

Kachina dolls (*Private collection*).

Anasazi pottery (*American Museum of Natural History, N.Y.*).

Hopi designs for women's shawls (*Private collection*).

Hopi basket designs (*Private collection*).

Bird designs from ancient Pueblo pottery *(Private collection)*.

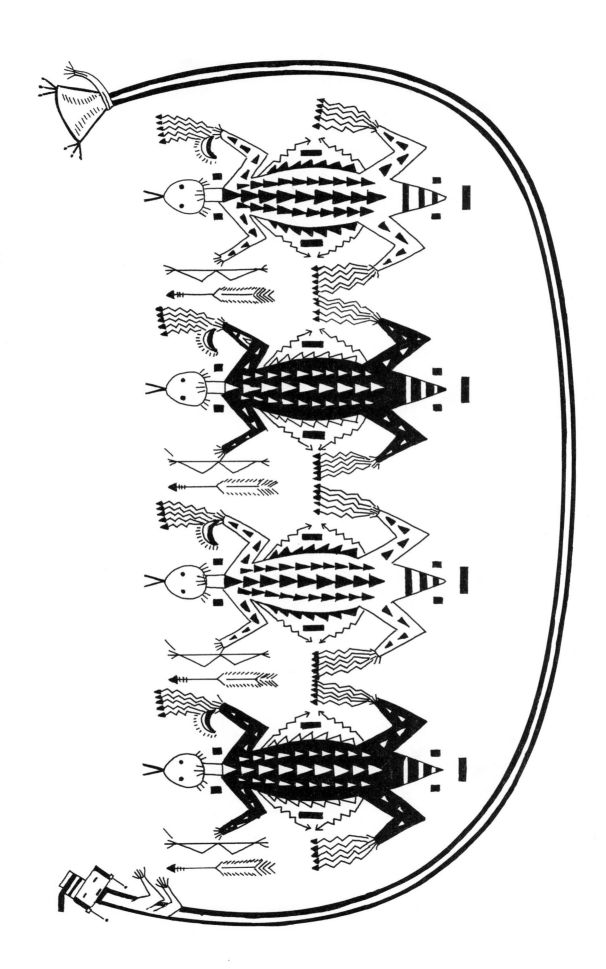

Navajo sand painting—Red Antway (*Wheelwright Museum of the American Indian, Santa Fe*).

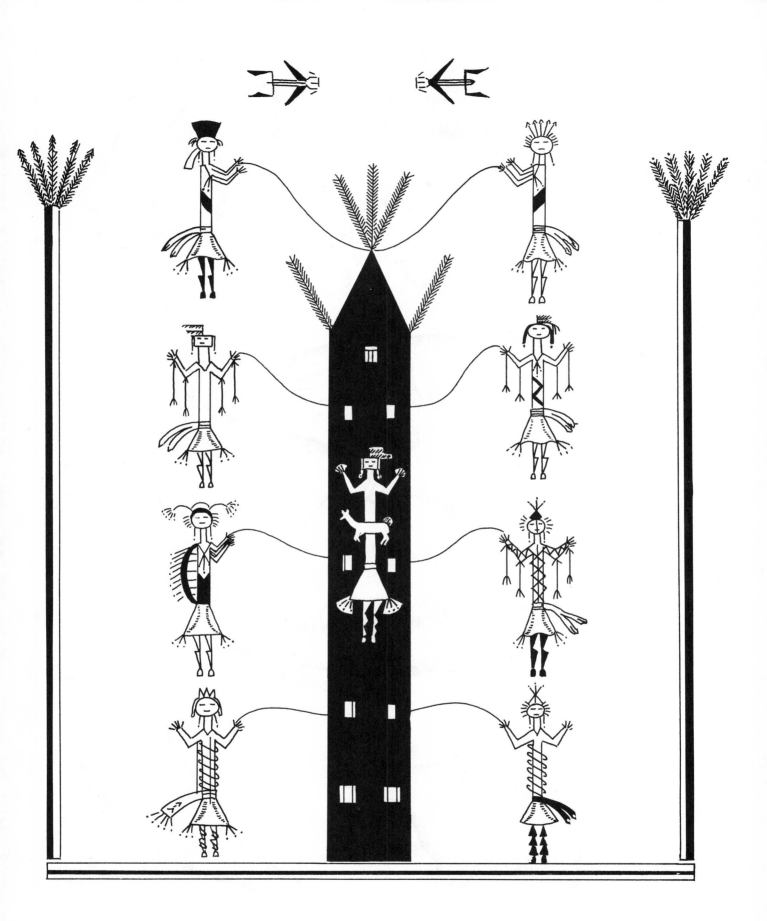

Navajo sand painting—Feather Chant, Rainbow, Flood, Yei saving tree
(*Wheelwright Museum of the American Indian, Santa Fe*).

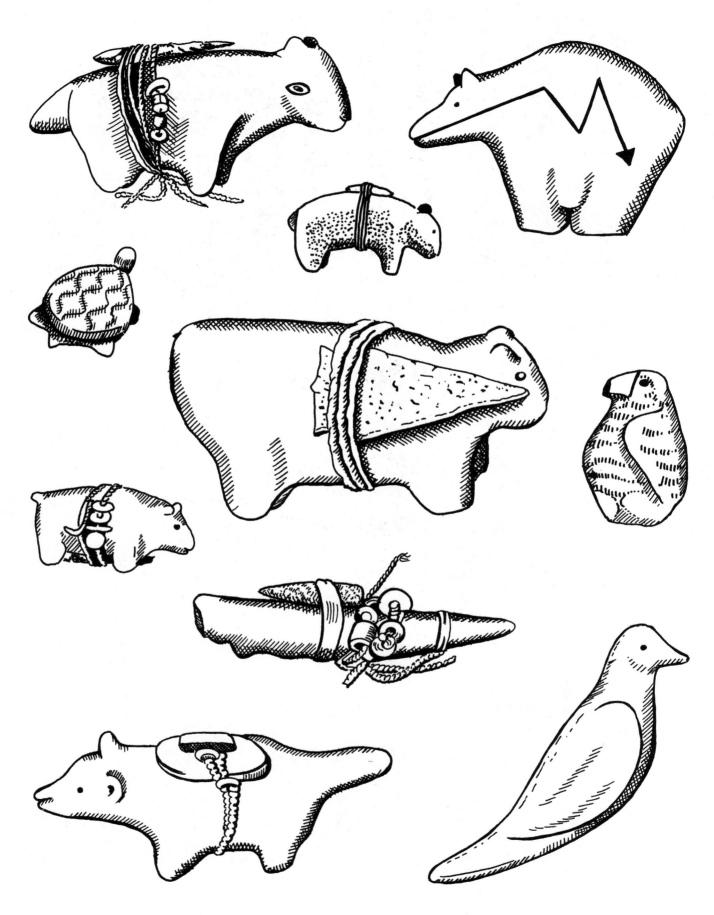

Zuni fetishes (*Private collection*).

TOP: Zuni masks. MIDDLE: Zia mask. BOTTOM: Zia mask and Zuni mask. (*Private collection*)

15

TOP: Zuni masks. MIDDLE: Navajo mask. BOTTOM: Navajo mask and Zuni mask. *(Private collection)*

16

Laguna drinking vessels *(Southwest Museum, Los Angeles; Museum of Indian Art and Culture, Santa Fe).*

Mimbres pottery art *(Maxwell Museum of Anthropology, Univ. of New Mexico, Albuquerque).*

Mimbres pottery designs *(Museum of the American Indian, Heye Foundation, N.Y.)*.

Navajo or Pueblo jewelry *(Museum of New Mexico, Santa Fe)*.

20

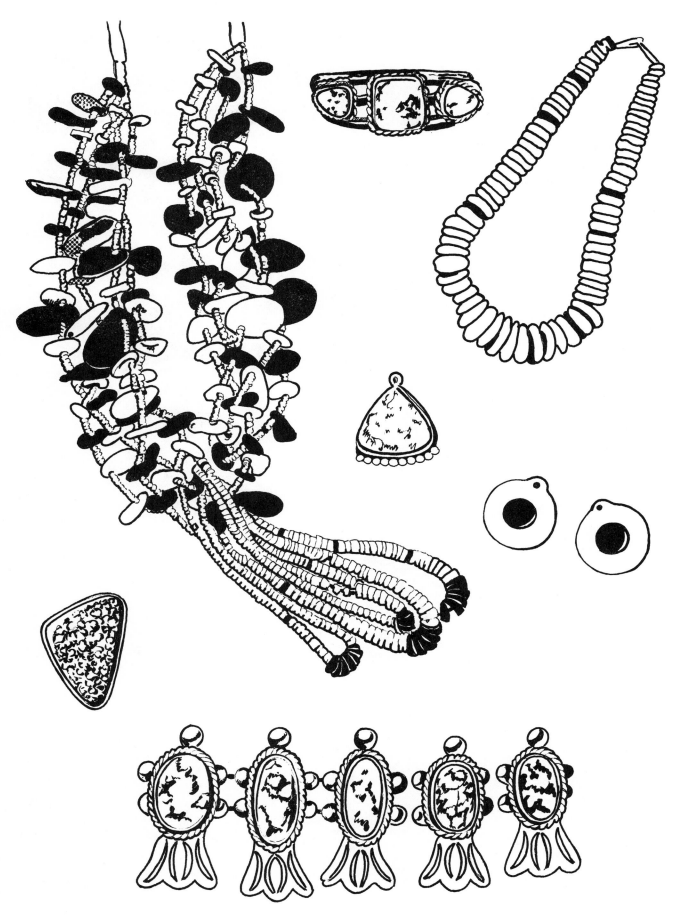

"Tab" necklace and other Navajo jewelry (*Millicent A. Rogers Museum, Taos, N.M.*).

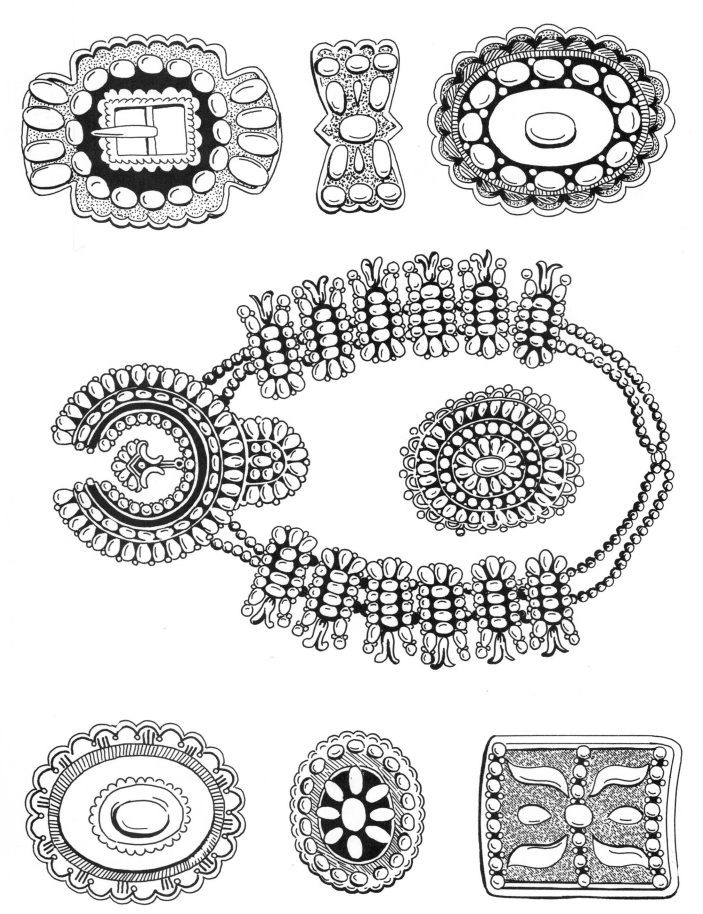

Pueblo and Navajo jewelry (*Millicent A. Rogers Museum, Taos, N.M.; Private collection*).

Navajo sand painting—Red Ant Chant. Woven border design.
(Wheelwright Museum of the American Indian, Santa Fe)

TOP: Navajo sand painting—Shooting Way. BOTTOM: Design from a beaded breastplate.
(Wheelwright Museum of the American Indian, Santa Fe)

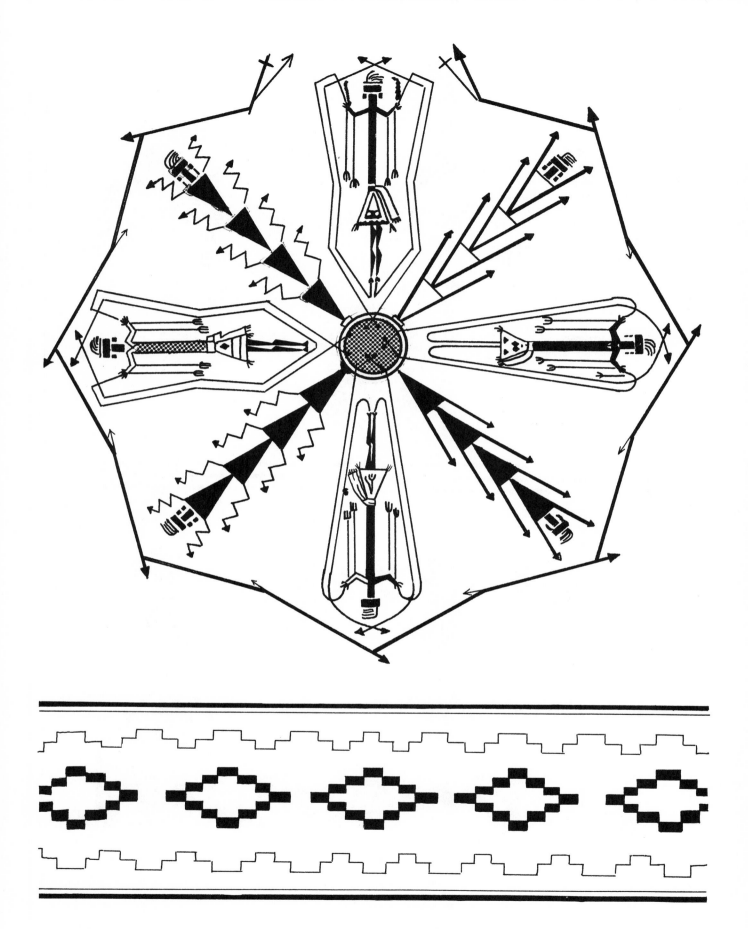

TOP: Navajo sand painting—Mountain Shooting Way. BOTTOM: Border design from woven shawl.
(*Wheelwright Museum of the American Indian, Santa Fe*)

25

Navajo sand painting—Sky, Earth, Eagles, Horned toad *(Wheelwright Museum of the American Indian, Santa Fe)*.

Anasazi art *(Peabody Museum of Archeology and Ethnology, Harvard Univ., Cambridge, Mass.;*
Museum of Indian Art and Culture, Santa Fe).

Hohokam art *(Museum of New Mexico, Santa Fe; Arizona State Museum, Univ. of Arizona, Tucson).*

Sikyatki pottery designs *(Southwest Museum, Los Angeles)*.

TOP: Zia slat altar. BOTTOM: Zia sand painting. *(Private collection)*

Zuni shields (*Museum of the American Indian, Heye Foundation, N.Y.*).

Cochiti pottery designs *(Southwest Museum, Los Angeles)*.

Pima basket designs *(Southwest Museum, Los Angeles)*.

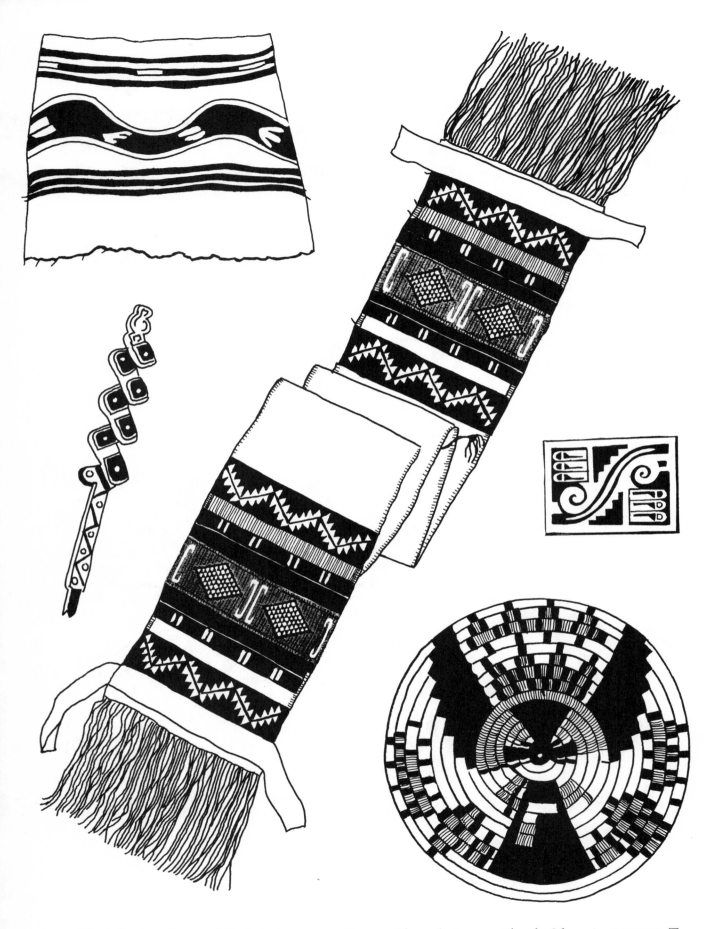

Hopi art. TOP: Ceremonial loincloth. MIDDLE: Ceremonial wand, Ceremonial sash, Silver pin. BOTTOM: Tray.

(Peabody Museum of Archeology and Ethnology, Harvard Univ., Cambridge, Mass.)

San Ildefonso pottery designs *(Museum of Indian Art and Culture, Santa Fe)*.

Acoma pottery designs *(Southwest Museum, Los Angeles)*.

Acoma pottery designs *(Southwest Museum, Los Angeles)*.

Papago basket designs *(Museum of Indian Art and Culture, Santa Fe)*.

Papago basket designs *(Museum of Indian Art and Culture, Santa Fe)*.

Santo Domingo pottery designs *(Southwest Museum, Los Angeles)*.

Apache basket and fiddle designs (*Museum of the American Indian, Heye Foundation, N.Y.*).

Kachina dolls (*American Museum of Natural History, N.Y.*).

TOP: Zuni dance wands. BOTTOM: Zuni pottery. (*American Museum of Natural History, N.Y.*)

Zia pottery designs *(Southwest Museum, Los Angeles)*.

Floral designs from Pueblo pottery *(Private collection).*

Floral designs from Pueblo pottery *(Private collection).*